EBBS
AND
FLOWS

A POETIC JOURNEY OF LIFE, LOVE, AND LOSS

KARLTON T. CLAY

Written By
Karlton T. Clay

Edited By
Karmen Scott

Photography By
Rita Mae Photography

Design By
Ashlee Henry

ABOUT THE AUTHOR

Karlton T. Clay, now introduced to the poetic world as *KayCee Thee Poet*, was born and raised in Augusta, Georgia. At the age of 16, Karlton was diagnosed with Acute Lymphoblastic Leukemia, but because of God's healing grace and mercy and with the medical expertise of the doctors and medical staff and the support of family and close friends, Karlton now stands strong as an 18-year cancer survivor.

Karlton graduated from John S. Davidson High School in 2004 and Georgia State University in Atlanta, Georgia in 2008. During his bout with cancer, Karlton was given the vision and the inspiration to begin his production company, Victory Productions. During his tenure, Karlton has produced several theatre productions, short films, and 15 web series totaling 377 episodes.

Karlton received a distribution deal with Maverick Movies in 2020 allowing him to turn his web series into a movie giving him the opportunity to produce his first feature-length film *Sweet Mahogany*, which now available on several major digital platforms.

In 2017, Karlton was named one of the Top 10 Young Professionals of Augusta by the Augusta Chamber of Commerce. In 2018, he was named one of Georgia's Top 40 Under 40 Professionals by Georgia Trend Magazine.

In everything he does, Karlton hopes to remain true to who he is and be that beacon of hope that will inspire others to follow their dreams. His motto: Grow as you go, which springs from his favorite scripture, "*I can do all things through Christ who strengthens me.*" Philippians 4:13

This collection of poetic consciousness is dedicated to the ones that were once loved and now are lost

and

To the loving memory of my sisters,

Kimberly Monique and Kristina Miracle Clay

and my grandparents,

Carlton and Georgia Louise Morris
and
Richard, Jr. and Ruby Louise Manor

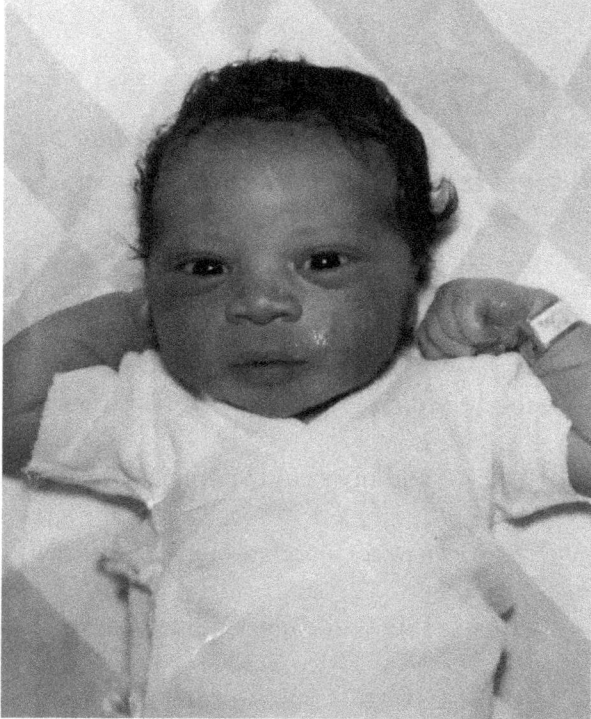

Baby ME!

JOB'S STORY

Inspired by the story of Job in the Bible (Job 1-2)

I guess God is trying to steal you away from me

He sent you to that church and He sat you down in that pew

He made you actually bring that big thick book of words written by Him

He made you actually bring a piece of paper and something to write with to take notes

Hey, no biggie

You'll read a few words and write down a couple of things

So what?

You'll eventually forget about it

I still have you

Wait a minute

You're actually starting to pay attention to that preacher

You're actually starting to praise and worship

You're actually starting to weep for your sins

But it's cool

You'll listen, praise, and cry

But you'll eventually not care anymore

I still have you

Wait a minute

That preacher is now offering Christ

He's telling you to come down the aisle and receive the love of Jesus

He's telling you that Jesus loves you and cares for you and wants to save you

Don't listen to him

He's lying

I'll sit in your lap though

I still have you

You have until tomorrow and many days after that

You have time

Don't get up

Wait a minute

You're actually standing

You're actually walking down the aisle

You're actually feeling sorry for every sin you've committed against God

You're actually praying the Prayer of Salvation and being real about it too

But you're just a kid

You don't understand what's going on

Maybe you do because you're smiling after you've finished praying

But I'm not worried

I'll get you back

I'm watching you

I'm thinking of ways to destroy you

See now you've switched sides

You think you're so special

You're saved

Spreading the word to the other so-called lost souls

You think you're some hot shot

You got your Heavenly Father on your side

Being blessed and prosperous and victorious

You think you're off-the-chain now

When you go through things, you have other believers in the faith to turn to

But I know you

I'm not concerned

I know the only reason why you worship God is because of how he's blessing you

I know it

I betcha if I were to go to God and tell Him you're just using Him that He'll make you suffer

God says that you're a good young man and would worship Him no matter what

But I beg to differ

God, I betcha if you quit blessing him and you bring sickness and harm to his body he'll curse your name in a hot second

I know it

I know him

God, how about you take that big ole' house away from his family

Make them move into a much, much smaller place

I bet he'll mock you then

He'll be disobedient and rebellious because he's put in a bad situation

And you say children obey your parents

I know he'll backslide

I know it

I know him

Do you give me permission to prove myself, God?

Good.

Let's see

What would make you doubt God?

I got it

How about cancerous cells that make you tired and sick and not able to praise God

How about something that'll make you not wanna pray and not wanna read the Bible

That's it

Now I got you

Now prove my point

Do it

I knew I'd still have you

Wait a minute

You're still smiling

You're still praying

You're still reading the Bible

You're still praising and worshipping God

What's going on?

I can't believe it

You actually have faith that God will deliver you from this

You're actually being a testimony to the doctors

A testimony to the nurses, your friends, and family

This is unbelievable

I thought I had you

I guess I was wrong

You do believe God can do all things

I guess you love God as much as you say you do

I guess I lost you

I guess I never had you

God, you were right

He cares for you

He worships you

He loves you

Senior Year of high school after battling cancer

YOU ARE PRECIOUS TO ME, YOU ARE HONORED, AND I LOVE YOU

Isaiah 43:4

When I lay on my bed and cry myself to sleep at night
"You are precious to me, You are honored, and I love you."
When I can't make a decision to determine wrong from right
"You are precious to me, You are honored, and I love you."
When I walk through life and I feel all alone
"You are precious to me, You are honored, and I love you."
When I need someone to talk to but no one picks up the phone
"You are precious to me, You are honored, and I love you."
When I slip and fall and give in to temptation
"You are precious to me, You are honored, and I love you."
When people all around me cause me constant aggravation
"You are precious to me, You are honored, and I love you."
When backbiting, hatred, and jealousy is all I see
"You are precious to me, You are honored, and I love you."
When anger, confusion, and sadness always want to consume me
"You are precious to me, You are honored, and I love you."
When good people do bad things and bad people are living good
"You are precious to me, You are honored, and I love you."
When sometimes I always feel misunderstood
"You are precious to me, You are honored, and I love you."
When some friends come and a lot of them go
"You are precious to me, You are honored, and I love you."

When those I love reject me with a non-subtle no

"You are precious to me, You are honored, and I love you."

When I look up to Heaven and You wipe my tears away

"You are precious to me, You are honored, and I love you."

When I cry out to You and I can FINALLY hear You say,

"You are precious to me, You are honored, and I love you."

NO ROOM TO COMPLAIN

I look in the mirror
And what do I see?
I can see clearly
How the Lord is blessing me

He gave me two legs and two arms
And two ears to hear
A mouth, nose, hands, and feet
And two eyes in order to see clear

As I look over my life,
I know I have favor and am blessed
Leukemia or any other disease
Could have had me in a coffin neatly dressed

When I look back over my life,
I see where the love of God has brought me from
His mercy and his grace is what is sustaining me
They will even until the Lord Jesus' return will come

As I looked on the news day after day,
I saw how New Orleans was covered with water
People lost their homes, jobs, and cars
Some even lost a parent, son, and/or daughter

I have some good days
And some bad ones, but who doesn't?
That could've been my body floating down a river
But by the grace of God, it wasn't

So whenever you or I have an urge
To whine about a bad grade or a pound you may gain
Just remember the victims and casualties of Hurricane Katrina
And you'll realize you have no room to complain

THANK YOU

Thank you for your patience
Thank you for your love
Thank you for always being there

Thank you for your commitment
Thank you for your voice
Thank you for showing that you care

Thank you for your words
Thank you for your corresponding action
Thank you for being on the team

Thank you for your prayers
Thank you for your gifts
Thank you for working towards the dream

Thank you for the encouraging gestures
Thank you for the encouraging songs
Thank you for the simple things: a smile and a nod

Thank you for having the right motives
Thank you for your love of the craft and the arts
Thank you for being obedient to God

Thank you for not doing it for the pay
Thank you for your faith that it's coming one day
Thank you for all that you do
Thank you for allowing me to take the time to say

THANK YOU

Me with my parents

MODERN DAY PHARISEES

Shaking my head at these modern day Pharisees
Talking a good game but the walk seems to disagree
So quick to use a verse to judge or criticize
But can you see the obvious pain in my eyes?

Shaking my head at these modern day Pharisees
You think you fancy huh because you now got a degree?
Not saying there is anything wrong with having a nice, house, money, or a car
But what about those you obviously ignore who are hurting around you and afar?

Shaking my head at these modern day Pharisees
Clearly caught up in your own ish to truly see
You seem more worried about your own day-to-day
Can't you take time to care for others and to pray?

Shaking my head at these modern day Pharisees
I guess I should just let you be
However, as I continue to write this poem, I am starting to see
That I need to truly look in the mirror because I am possibly shaking my head at *me*

ODE TO THE UNCOMMITTED

I'm tired of the phonies and the flakes
The pretenders and the fakes
Who ain't willing to do what it takes
To work hard and make history

Speakin' life with yo' mouth but yo' actions speak anotha
You actin' a lil' shady... are you workin' undercova
You supposed to have my back and I'm 'posed to call you sis or brotha
Yet your commitment to the cause is still a mystery

We supposed to be in this together and work as a team
We supposed to be pushin', grindin', and strivin' for da same dream
But now you don't care, you won't fight, and you seem
To always cast me aside like it don't matter

You don't show up, you don't call, you don't let no one know
That you don't wanna chase the dream anymo'
"I ain't gotta put my all into it or do it especially since I ain't gettin' no dough"
I bet you'd be more enthused if it made your pockets fatter

Dreams are shattered, feelings are hurt, emotions on the run
People are tired, fed up, or no longer having fun
God is forsaken and forgotten about and now we're done
Forgetting why we committed to this in the first place

Discouraged, angry, sad, confused

Hurting, crying, sighing, no longer amused

Feelings of doubt, despair, or feeling misused

Don't know if I can even finish this race.....

No more self-pity, now I gotta lift my head up

The Lord promised He will always fill my cup

I will not stop, I will not quit, from His Power I will sup

I gotta put my trust in Him and stop being so dim-witted

Thank You Lord for giving me the strength to keep going

Thank You for blessing me with true warriors with their talents and gifts they are sowing

You are the One removing the phonies, flakes, and fakes, and like the wind away they are blowing

And with this I present to you the ode to the uncommitted

INTERRUPTIONS

Whenever I
> *Shut up and listen to what I have to say*

Try to talk
> *My way is the right way*

To you or give
> *Listen to me*

My opinion about our
> *I'm always right*

Conversation, you always seem
> *You're wrong*

To cut me off
> *You're always wrong*

Or deem what I have
> *No one cares*

To say as unimportant
> *Everyone should always think how I think*

Or invaluable
> *Everyone should feel how I feel*

You make me feel
> *My opinion is better than yours*

Uncomfortable and I can't
> *Who cares about what you think*

Deal with talking
> *You're never right about anything*

To you right
> *Blah, blah, blah*

Now until you stop
> *I can't hear you*

Interrupting me and
> *Come on. You know I'm right*

Listen to and comprehend
> *What I have to say is ten times better than what you have to say*

14

What I have

Are you still talking?

To say

NEGATIVITY

Tired of all the negativity
Started to suck away my creativity
I understand that it's nothing but the enemy
Using those around to be against me

Should I fuss?
No.
Should I cuss?
No.
Should I stay?
Yes.
Should I pray?
Yes?

Should I say what's on my mind?
Maybe.
Should I continue to be kind?
Okay, let's see.

Tired of all the hypocrisy
Talking behind each other's backs is all I see
No one around for good company
Discouraging me from being all I can be

Should I scream?

No.

Should I shout?

No.

Should I cry?

No.

Should I pout?

No.

Should I continue to be humble?

Yes.

Admit when I stumble?

Yes.

Never crumble...

Yes.

Negativity... Hypocrisy... The Enemy... All I see... is me.

LIFE GOES ON

Hello, Goodbye
We laugh, We cry
You Live, You Die
Life Goes On

Ebbs and Flow
I Stop, You Go
Some Come, Most Go
Life Goes On

Stand or Bow
There's Later, There's Now
Some ask Why, Others ask How
Life Goes On

Chaos or Zen
We lose, We Win
Old Chapters Close, New Ones Begin
Life Goes On

I Smile, I Cry
I know How, but I'll never know Why
Sometimes I Live wishing I would Die
But yet still... Life Goes On

WHY?

When traveling down the road of life
Different obstacles may go by
We sometimes find ourselves
Asking God "Why?"

Why must the ones we love die?
Why must there be pain in life?
Why must we have sorrow?
Why hope for tomorrow?
Why must we shed a tear?
Why does what happens is what we fear?
Why are the clouds always blocking the sun?
Why can't life always be happiness and fun?

It's not wrong to ask questions like those
I'm assuming that that's normal, I suppose
When your life is full of heartbreak and scorn
And you feel like what's the point of being born
Trusting in the Lord is the best road to travel by
He's always with you even when you're wondering why

ANY DAY NOW

In Memory Of My Grandmommy, Georgia Louise Morris

Any day now I know that you are going to leave me here

Any day now I know that you will no longer be around to hold me near

Any day now I will no longer hear those stories that are embarrassing and old

Any day now I know my fears of you departing will quickly unfold

Any day now you'll breathe your last breath in this place

Any day now you will finally complete your earthly race

Any day now that day will come and go

Any day now you'll look down from Heaven at me on earth below

Any day now you'll be with The Life, The Truth, and The Way

Any day now we'll be reunited some day

REMINISCE

In Memory Of My Grandmommy, Georgia Louise Morris

Patt-a-cake, patt-a-cake

Oh how I miss the way the house would smell of the wonderful things you would bake

The adventures and lessons that you told

The way your kisses warmed me up in the cold

"Remember in Hawaii when you hit me with that yellow bat?"

I always use to protest, "I don't remember that."

Can't forget that chair in the corner by the microwave

And you never would hesitate to pull out that belt to make us behave

The way you sat me in your lap and held me in your arms

In order to protect me from the world's harms

I always have and will feel comforted in hour presence

Always reminding me of God's omnipresence

Y&R... I think you were the one that got me hooked

Introducing me to fried gizzards, chitlins, pig feet, ox tails, and other things uniquely cooked

Crossword puzzles and coffee with cream

Burgundy lipstick and a smile with a beam

I love you and miss you and sitting on your knee

That's going to do for... grandmommy and me!

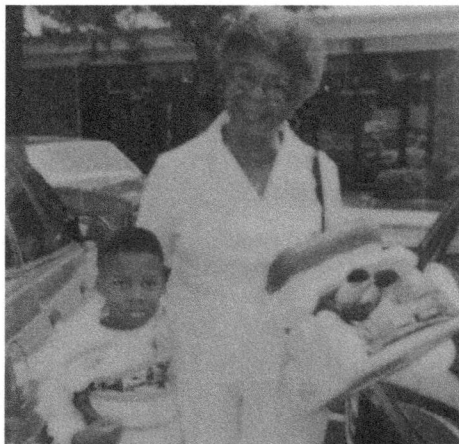

My Grandmother
Georgia Louise Morris

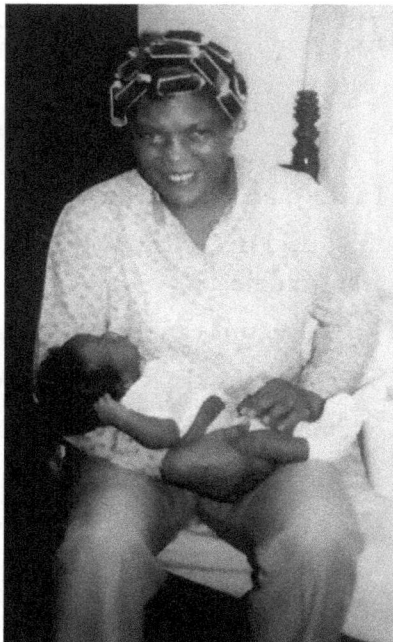

My Grandmother
Ruby Manor

My Grandfather
Carlton Morris

My Grandfather
Richard Manor, Jr.

LEAVING YOUR LEGACY

Dedicated to the memory and life of my granddaddy, Carlton Morris

I remember always wanting to be around you
I remember you always loving me
I remember your kind and encouraging words
I didn't realize then that you were leaving a legacy

I remember the way you entered a room
I remember you letting me sit on your knee
I remember the way you shook my hand
I didn't realize then that you were leaving a legacy

I remember always wondering why you called me Tyrone
I remember always wondering why you had the same first name as me
I remember always anxious to learn our history
I didn't realize then that you were leaving a legacy

I remember the way you loved your wife
I remember the way you embraced my siblings and me
I remember the way you took care of your daughters
I didn't realize then that you were leaving a legacy

I remember how proud you were of my accomplishments
I remember how you always were concerned about me
I remember how you listened and gave us your wisdom
I didn't realize then that you were leaving a legacy

There will never be another man like you
I'm happy that you shared your name with me
Now that you are gone, I will always miss you
But through us... you will continue to leave your legacy

JUST CAN'T FIND THE WORDS

I just can't find the words to say
I miss you doesn't seem to be enough
I just can't find the words to say
My love for you is making this transition tough

I just can't find the words to say
In my mind when I see your face
I just can't find the words to say
When what was once full is now an empty space

I just can't find the words to say
When I want to pray but my faith starts to waiver
I just can't find the find the words to say
Even though I know you are now with our Savior

I just can't find the words to say
When I want you here
I just can't find the words to say
When I know that you're no longer near

I just can't find the words to say
When I'm always asking "Why?"
I just can't find the words to say
I wasn't ready to say goodbye

I just can't find the words to say
When all I can do is sigh
I just can't find the words to say
And all I want to do is cry

I just can't find the words to say
And I'm trying to be strong
I just can't find the words to say
With you is where I want to belong

In my head, it makes sense
I know we will see her again one day
But in my heart, it's breaking
Because I just can't find the words to say

WORDS OF ENCOURAGEMENT

Matthew 5:4; 28:19-20; Ecclesiastes 2:4; 1 Corinthians 4:24-27;
1 Peter 1:23; Philippians 1:21; 4:4

Death

A word that most of us dread

We are born

We live and fulfill our purpose

We die

And life continues

How do we deal with the pain?

Does God even care?

Of course because He comforts those that mourn

Weep for we have lost someone we love

Laugh for we remember the good times

Mourn for we respect his remembrance

Dance for he's in heaven with our Lord

Life is a race

Our prize is an incorruptible crown

Through Christ we have been born again

To live is to fulfill our purpose

Spread the gospel

Share Christ in love

Teach the lost

And obey His commands

To die is to live with Him in Heaven forever

So rejoice in the Lord always

He reigneth forever

And one day we all will be with Him

So if you want to cry

Cry

If you want to weep

Weep

If you want to laugh

Laugh

If you want to dance

Dance

If you want to pray

Pray

If you want to praise

Praise

Whatever you do

Wherever you go

Whatever you say

Just remember that he's with Christ today

My Sister
Kimberly Monique Clay

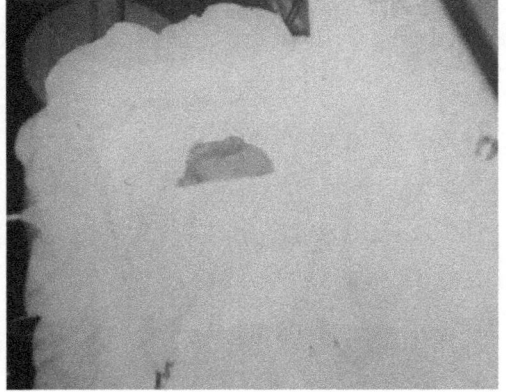

My Sister
Kristina Miracle Clay

Me with my siblings

WAITING AND WATCHING

Waiting and watching.... watching and waiting
Sitting with unanswered questions anticipating

How did this happen? What exactly went wrong?
Why does life throw you the same tune to a different song?

What are the alternatives? Could I have done something differently?
What are we supposed to learn? What exactly am I supposed to see?

What can I do to make this pain go away?
Is my faith starting to waiver? How am I supposed to pray?

Is this a trial? Is it a test? Is my faith supposed to grow?
Should I already have the answers? How am I supposed to know?

My questions are unanswered....my thoughts are unclear
Silently.... quietly.... continuing to anxiously sit here

Mind moving fast....internally debating
As I continue to sit in silence.... watching and waiting

MY FIRST HEARTBREAK

I thought you loved me
I thought you cared
I thought you were faithful
To be secure with when I'm scared

When I first saw you
I knew I had to be careful
I slowly approached you
'Cause I knew you were special

We hooked up and was happy
We laughed and talked on the phone
I thought I couldn't live without you
I never wanted to be alone

We started having problems
But we always worked it out
Either by talking or writing
Or we'd have to yell, scream, or shout

You always had my back
You were there when I became ill
You loved and cared for me
I knew what we had was real

But then something happened
Something not so great
We just quit communicating
Breaking up was our fate

But before our departure
You hurt me deep in my heart
You talked about me behind my back
You tore my heart apart

Dudes want to fight me
And tear me in two
They mock me and hate me
All of this because of you

I'm saddened and dismayed
Hurt and angry
But I can't seem to do anything about it
I'm in pain, don't you see?

You were my first love
My very special girl
My one and only sweetheart
As precious as a pearl

But now we're no longer together
Don't know how much I can take
We're not even friends
And this was my first heartbreak

GIVEN UP ON LOVE

Have I given up on love?
I don't know what I'm feelin'
I know my heart is aching
From constant rejection from women

Have I given up on love?
My heart is starting to get cold
Fear begins to set in
Of never finding the one of who I'll grow old

Have I given up on love?
Taking a look at my life
Trying to figure out if
I've ever caused anyone hurt or strife

Have I given up on love?
Trying to look to the future
Finding a young lady I like
But me not having what will suit her

Have I given up on love?
Trying to live in the present
But her disinterest in me
Is obviously more apparent

Have I given up on love?
Maybe. I dunno.
The constant rejection

What point is my heart fo'?

Have I given up on love?
It's becoming a reality
Starting to ask questions
What's da matter with me?

Have I given up on love?
I guess that's what it may seem
Picking away at my heart
Picking away at my self-esteem

Have I given up on love?
Seeing everyone so happy
What have I done
To make my love life so crappy?

Have I given up on love?
Consuming myself with my career
I just want someone to hold me close
And say, "I love you, dear."

Have I given up on love?
I don't wanna run out of time
I want someone who'll love me for me
Not for my potential coming dime

The love that's sustaining me
Seems to be sent from above
It's the only thing that's keeping me
From giving up on love

FOR A BRIEF MOMENT IN TIME

For A Brief Moment In Time
You were able to open my eyes
I saw you for who you really are
What was once dead inside begin to rise

For A Brief Moment In Time
My feelings were not ignored
My heart was able to feel again
My love for you suddenly soared

For A Brief Moment In Time
You allowed me inside
What we felt for one another
We no longer had to hide

For A Brief Moment In Time
That look in your eyes gave me a sign
That my heart belonged to yours
And your soul connected with mine

For A Brief Moment In Time
Your words were so loving and kind
What I anticipated for finally happened
You made love to my body and my mind

For A Brief Moment In Time
We let go and let it be
Our realities did not exist
Our world was only you and me

For A Brief Moment In Time
I whispered the words I love you
And by the way you kissed me
I could tell that you love me too

For A Brief Moment In Time
My longtime friend became my lover at the drop of a dime
I'll forever hold on to what we shared
Even if it was only For A Brief Moment In Time

ALMOST BEEN A YEAR

It's almost been a year

Since the devil used you to try and kill me, destroy me, and annihilate me

It's almost been a year

Since I was held in captivity by your bondage

It's almost been a year

Since you manipulated me for your own purposes

It's almost been a year

Since I was foolish enough to hurt and disobey my God to please you

It's almost been a year

Since I doubted who I was

It's almost been a year

Since I continued to make the same stupid mistakes

It's almost been a year

Since I said no more

It's almost been a year

Since I stopped living that double, destructive life

It's almost been a year

Since I made a commitment to purity

It's almost been a year

Since I cut you out completely

It's almost been a year

Since I tried to compress my hate for you

It's almost been a year

Since even though you ruined my life, I was commanded to still love you
with God's love

I never want to see you again
And I've made that very clear
But it still hurts to think about
Even though it's almost been a year

GET OFF ME

Get off me! Leave me alone!
I'm tired of you trying to drag me down
You are trying to distract me
Distorting my vision of my goals and ultimately a Heavenly crown

I wish I never met you
I wish I never had to deal with your nonsense
I try to erase you and keep you in the past
But it seems you try and creep up in the present tense

Get off me! Leave me alone!
I hate you; don't ever come back
You're trying to stop me from pursuing my dreams
You're trying to throw me off track

You're a liar! I'm not like that anymore
So stop feeding me these lies
You whisper sweet nothings in my ear
But your voice I terribly despise

Get off me! Leave me alone!
I want to erase you completely from my memory
You're poison: despicable and dreadful
You are definitely no good to me

I cry to God to help and deliver me
And I already know that He has
But why do you keep bothering me?
Why don't you just go on and pass?

Get off me! Leave me alone!
Why did you choose to mess with me?
I have nothing you want
Please just let me be

I'm walking in a new light: God's grace and mercy
So I will no longer pick at this bone
So I'm not going to tell you again
Get off me and leave me alone!

I BET YOU THINK POEM IS ABOUT YOU

You messed with my Mental
Made me question the Spiritual
Retract the Physical and abandon the Emotional
So now it's time for me to get Lyrical

As I step in front of your lens,
Recognize that it's my time to cleanse
So if what I have to say does offend
Then maybe you should check yourself so you can comprehend

Now before you get caught up,
I'll have you seething like hot coffee from a cup
I bet you think these words are about you?
You're so vain... so of course you do.

Yes, I've been sippin'
But it was you who was trip-trippin'
Looking me in the soul of my eyes
Pretending to be an angel in disguise

I finally had an epiphany
That you actually bring out the worse in me
See, you're actually a wolf in sheep's clothing
Taking advantage of all who you're devouring

I bet you think these lyrics are about you
As you try to worm your way through The Who's who
Always making me feel like I'm in the wrong
As you continue killing me softly with that same ole song

You speak with ambiguity
Making folks think you walk with honor and integrity
But this is a no flex zone so you can quit pretending, too
Because baby, I now know the real you

So as I work on having no more drama in my life
I'm done with all of your pain and all of your strife
So now I bet you think this poem is about you
Well, it is... so what you gonna do?

SCORNED

Manipulator
Violator
Agitator
Puppet Master

You pulled the strings of my thoughts and feelings manipulating how I feel
Making me climb a wall of impossible expectations that seemed so unreal
Belittling me with your words but I don't seem to mind
An invitation into your heart and inner most thoughts was what I was hoping to find

Your presence, your aura, your energy - all so intoxicating
Connecting with your body and your soul was what I was once craving
Making me feel that maybe one day we can have it all
But once I let go of my inhibitions, you put up that wall

Lost... Afraid... Not really sure what to say
Scared to say how I feel; scared to throw it all away
Life's too short for what ifs and could be
If I can get over that wall, you and I can be a possibility

Ok, here we go; it's either now or never
What I am about to say could change things forever
As I look you in your eyes and try to connect to your heart
I say how I feel hoping you'll do your part

Pouring out the issues of my heart was not an easy task
But I know that I could no longer wear this mask
A sigh of relief as I await what you have to say
As if my hopes and dreams would come alive today

However, disappointment begins to set in
As I begin to feel you close yourself back up from within
Looking at me like I did something wrong
Now I'm beginning to hear the melody to a familiar song

"I see you as a friend; I don't want to ruin that"
"We work together; let's keep our business intact"
"You read it wrong; I don't like you like that"
"Naw, I'm good on you, but you still a cool cat"

It's coming true - my nightmare and my fears
Trying to get a hold of myself before you see the tears
Oh, it's too late... you have seen me cry
The only question left in this equation is why

You preyed upon my loneliness and my insecurities
You played with my heart making me feel like I had no worries
My vision of you now is starting to get hazy
As you flip the script making me feel like what I feel is crazy

Walking on eggshells not to make you mad
But you stomped all over my heart which makes me more than sad
Making me live up to all of these expectations just to be around you
Never felt good enough to be invited into your crew

A picture is worth a thousand words - I guess it's true what they say

Now when I see you, all I can remember is the sadness in my eyes from that day

When you made me feel ugly, less than, and worthless

Now that I know where we stand, I no longer have to guess

You're a slick son of a gun making me think this is all my fault

Making me feel like I'm the only responsible for things coming to a screeching halt

The rose colored glasses have been taken off and over you I will no longer cry

I guess the last thing for this scorned heart to say to you, manipulator, violator, agitator, puppet-master, is goodbye

ABC'S

You say you want nothing to do with me with your words but your actions speak a different tune

You say you don't want to ruin the friendship but you're so quick to walk away from it every new moon

You say I'm not keeping it real or simple so let me break it down

Let me take you through the journey of my feelings with the ABC's sound

Abandoned because I'm feeling

Betrayed which has me feeling kind of

Chaotic because you

Devastated me making me feel

Excluded and now I'm acting

Foolish because I feel like

Garbage which makes me feel

Hurt,

Ignored,

Jaded, and

Kicked-down because I'm just plain

Lonely and so now you have

Mistreated me and

Neglected me causing me to feel

Oppressed and I can no longer hide this

Pain but I must stay

Quietly angry even though I feel

Rejected,

Shame,

Turmoil,

Ugly,

Vengeful, and

Worthless all at the same time so I'm

Xtremely Depressed which leads to Plain Ole

Yuck Because YOU took the

Zealousness from my heart with your words and your actions

So... now you know my ABCs,

Next time will you please stop hurting me?

REAL TALK

You abandoned me, you neglected me
You let go of my hand
You used me, you abused me
With all of my love, even still I understand

I support you, I encourage you
I promised that I'd never leave your side
I cherish you, I will forever love you
I was always there with a shoulder when you cried

Sometimes it seems like you don't really appreciate me
Even after everything that I have done
Sometimes it feels like you don't even like me
I said I'll always be your friend even though you act like you have none

I have to be honest it hurts when my love isn't reciprocated
Because my heart is so big and my love for you is so wide
I have to be honest it hurts when my trust and adoration isn't received
Because I often feel like my wish for you to be with me is often denied

I want to be there for you, I want to comfort you and hold you
But it seems like you often push me away
I want to care for you, I want to love all up on you
But it appears that from me you would rather go astray

Nevertheless, I will always be here
No matter what you say or do or how you act
Because my love for you will always be unconditional
Nothing or no one can change that fact

Meditate. Pray. Think. Listen. Learn.
Watch. Seek. Ask. Receive. Look in the mirror and see.
Now understand that this is God doing the talking
And after listening, I suddenly realized He was talking about... **ME.**

The Future
My Nephew and Niece - Kyler Terrell and Kimberly Alise